My Bible Study Journal

Making the Scriptures Practical

Tokunbo O. Okulaja

All rights reserved. This book is protected by the copyright laws of the United States of America. This book may not be copied or reprinted for commercial gain or profit. No copies of this book or any parts of this book can be reprinted or disseminated in any form including- electronic, mechanical, photocopy, recording, or otherwise unless you have prior written permission from the publisher- TTL Publishing. Permission will be granted upon request.

My Bible Study Journal: Making the Scriptures Practical
TTL Publishing
P.O. Box 1744
Wake Forest, North Carolina 27588
info@tokunbotheleader.com

Visit the author's website at tokunbotheleader.com.

Cover Design by Adriane Racquel Creative.

Unless otherwise noted, all scriptures are taken from the New King James Version of the Bible.

My Bible Study Journal: Making the Scriptures Practical/ Tokunbo O. Okulaja.
ISBN: 978-1-7378576-6-2

This Journal belongs to

_____

STARTED ON

_____

Introduction

One of the ways that God communicates to His children is through the Word of God. The Word of God is essential for you to grow as a Believer. It is up to you to decide to do a deep dive analysis into the scriptures to discover God's character, nature, and heart. In addition, the Bible should be used to help you discover your identity, purpose, and destiny in God.

The Bible is not a storybook or random words in a book. God's Word was meant for you to learn how to look and behave more like Him. The scriptures are alive and active (Hebrews 4:12). The pages in the Bible are waiting on you to discover more about God and yourself.

This journal is intended for you to study the scriptures. Learning how to study the Bible can be a daunting task. With this journal, go with God at your own pace to discover jewels about the kingdom of God. Studying enables you to look intricately at every passage to discover God's heart for his people. When you study the scriptures, you look for the interpretation of the original meaning of the Scriptures.

You have chosen to go on this journey of making the scriptures practical because you desire to know God in a deeper way. In your heart, you know that there are so many realms to God that you have yet to discover. May this journal and your hunger for studying unlock you into a place of going into higher heights and deeper depths with your Father.

Bible Study Goals

One of the ways that you're going to be motivated to continue to actively study the Word of God is by setting goals. There are numerous ways to decide how you will read the scriptures. You can choose to set a goal for the year, month, or day. Have a conversation with the Holy Spirit to identify the goal that He has for you around studying the scriptures. Whenever you get weary or bored, bring yourself back to your goals for the year. In addition, if you lose focus throughout the year, come back to this part of your journal to remind yourself of where God wants to take you.

Directions: Read the following topics of study that people decide to do more research on using the scriptures. Choose how you want to study the Bible with God throughout the year. You can change your goals as the Holy Spirit leads you. How you decide to study the Bible will impact the scriptures that you decide to read for that day. Have at least one area you want to focus on when you are participating in a Bible study session. Always strive to study the scriptures with a purpose from God. Ultimately, studying the scriptures should help you learn more about God, Jesus, the Holy Spirit, yourself, and the world.

Create a Plan (these are suggestions)

1. **Study the Bible by a topic of interest.** For example, you can state that you want to study the Bible about faith, salvation, deliverance, healing, leadership, miracles, etc.
2. **Authors/biblical characters**: You want to learn more about Isaiah, Ezekiel, Apostle Paul, etc. for some reason. Write down the names of biblical characters that you want to study and what scriptures need to be studied to understand these individuals.
3. Books of the Bible. For example, you can complete a study on Proverbs once a day for a month or year. A study on the Book of Psalms.
4. Jesus' ministry
5. Certain time-frames or locations (geography)
6. The nature of God
7. The Gospels
8. Bible in a year plan
9. Alphabetical order or traditional order of the Bible
10. Old Testament
11. New Testament

You can choose to create your own goals/strategies that are not listed here.

Strategize

In the boxes provided, write down the topics you want to study and the goals that you have for each month. Be sure to pray with God to ask Him what will be beneficial for you to study at this point in your life and why it is important. Having a <u>strategy</u> for reading your Bible will keep you focused throughout the year.

Month	January	February	March	April
Topic/Strategy **Example: I will study The Gospels.**				
Why do you want to study this topic?				
What days will you study the Bible for 30 minutes or more?				

Month	May	June	July	August
Topic/ Strategy **Example: I will study The Gospels**				
Why do you want to study this topic?				
What days will you study the Bible for 30 minutes or more?				

Month	September	October	November	December
Topic/ Strategy **Example: I will study The Gospels.**				
Why do you want to study this topic?				
What days will you study the Bible for 30 minutes or more?				

Bible Study Reading Tips

Many people decide not to study the scriptures mainly because they say they do not have enough time. Studying the Bible goes beyond casually reading or meditating. As a Believer, you should strive to read the Bible every single day. Reading the Bible can be something casual where you open up the scriptures for about 5 to 20 minutes to simply hear from God. When it comes to studying the Bible, this means that you take about 30 minutes to an hour or even more to discover more about God. This is the time when you take out your dictionary, maps, history books, encyclopedias, commentaries, etc. to discover the deeper meaning behind His Word.

Do not allow excuses to hinder you from being a person that studies the scriptures. In 2 Timothy 2:15 God challenges all Believers to be people that study the word of God, a workman that need not be ashamed rightly dividing the word of Truth. If you have a busy schedule and you cannot commit to studying the Bible every day, choose at least two to three days out of the week where you will sit down with God to study the Word. Choose specific times on your calendar to meet with God to study the Bible.

If you are a kingdom leader (leader in the body of Christ) or in your church, it is going to be important for you to study the scriptures at least 4 to 5 times a week. There is a greater expectation for you to be a person that studies so that you can provide people with spiritual wisdom. Create a routine that is best for you so that you can be well acquainted with God's instructions.

You should also use a Bible that you can understand. There are a plethora of Bible translations that you can connect with to keep you motivated to study your Bible. Also, invest in getting a Bible that you can annotate or take notes in.

Another way to keep you motivated to read the scriptures is to start with reading the New Testament. You may understand the Old Testament better if you first start with reading the book of John first or any of the Gospels. Also, if your church offers a Bible study time, make it a point to attend the Bible study meeting.

Find a placid environment that gives you the ability to focus on the scriptures. Choose a place to study the Bible that gives you peace of mind. Lastly, obtain any resources that you need, whether it be a cool highlighter, flashcards, colorful pens, dictionaries, etc. so that you can stay focused on meeting with God to study the Bible.

Feed My Sheep

In John 21:17, Jesus tells Peter that if He loves Jesus that Peter must feed Jesus' sheep. Peter was a leader that was charged with taking care of God's people. If you are a leader of God's people, you have the same commandment that was given to Peter: feed His sheep.

Change your perspective about studying the Bible by embracing the fact that God has chosen you to feed His sheep. Because He chose you to feed His sheep, He will help you on your journey of decoding the meaning of the Word of God. You can only feed His sheep if you consume His word. The greatest way to give your audience spiritual sustenance and nutrients is by reading the scriptures. What you teach people as a leader in the body of Christ must be rooted in what the Bible conveys. The Bible is a Believer's compass. It is the navigation system that Believers use to live lives that are pleasing to the Father.

Do a deep dive analysis to understand and uncover the instructions that God has given His people to live lives that will honor him. If you love God and His people, feed His sheep with spiritual wisdom, knowledge, and understanding.

Allaying Our Fears

One of the reasons why people do not study the scriptures is because they do not want to get it wrong. When you first start off reading the Bible, it can be a daunting endeavor. However, if you are consistent and you deeply desire for the Holy Spirit to reveal Jesus to you through the scriptures, God will meet you in your desires. Simply giving up and not taking out the time to discover the many sides of God through the scriptures will not allow you to mature as a Believer.

When you come to the scriptures, no matter how many years that you have been studying the Bible, you still need to come to the scriptures with a heart of humility. Many people study the Bible for years and they still discover that they know nothing. When you resolve that you know absolutely nothing, then God can meet you to show you all things about Him.

Do not grow puffed-up in the knowledge that you understand from the scriptures. Your motivation or prayer should always be: God show me more about Jesus and show me more about myself through the scriptures. If you are a leader of any organization, begin to ask God to show you about your community, your family, and other endeavors via the Word of God.

Choosing a Bible

There are many versions of the Bible that you can choose to use for your personal growth. Choose a version of the Bible that allows you to understand what God is expressing. If you are not accustomed to King Jame's English, classic Bible versions that people start with are the New International Version (NIV), English Standard Version (ESV), or New Living Translation (NLT). If you purchase the Amplified Bible, there will be some Hebrew and Greek words defined for you in parenthesis. You can decide to use different versions of the same scriptures for you to get an enhanced meaning of what God has spoken.

If you are new to the journey of studying the scriptures, you should invest in a study Bible or life application study Bible. These Bibles typically contain commentaries, historical facts, maps, charts, etc. that can help you stay invested in studying the Word.

You can also choose to listen to the audio version of the Bible via the Bible application or online materials. Search online for the audio versions of your favorite versions of the Bible.

How to Use this Bible Study Journal

As was mentioned earlier, you can choose to study the Bible based on books, themes, characters/figures, alphabetical order, traditional Bible order, etc. Each journal entry in this tool gives you the space to write out your thoughts for the day concerning a particular passage.

Before *you start each day, say the prayer provided or create your own. Say:* *Holy Spirit, I invite You into this Bible study time. Holy Spirit please illuminate Your wisdom where there are dark places. I come before You to say that I know nothing without the Holy Spirit, and I believe that You can show me all things. During this time, keep my mind focused on studying the scriptures. Remove every impediment that would try to distract me from spending time with You today. In Jesus' name, I pray, Amen!*

There are seven sections to each journal entry. Each day you're going to be challenged to write out a **focus question, observations, interpretation, general application, personal application, action steps,** and **prayer**.

***Refer back to these pages for more information when you are completing your journal entry for the day.

Introduction: Focus/Research Question
You can come up with a focus/research question after you have read the scriptures for the day. Also, you can choose to simply write out the topic that you want to focus on for the day. When you are completing the interpretation section, you can focus your research on your research question/topic for the day. [*****While studying, allow the Holy Spirit to guide and shift you as He sees fit.**]

1. Observation Section
The first step to studying the Bible is simply doing an observation!

In this section look for the following sections listed below. Your job is to not find meaning, but note what it is that you simply see after reading.
1. What do you notice at first glance about the section you are reading?
2. What names were introduced?
3. What do you notice about the setting?
4. What words are repeated?
5. What words stood out to you?
6. Who is involved in these scriptures?
7. What questions do you have after reading this section?
8. What questions do you have about God, Jesus, and the Holy Spirit?
9. Where are the events that took place?
10. What mood do you have after reading this section?

2. Interpretation

The second step to studying the Bible is interpreting or discovering the original intent of the scriptures read. Some scholars refer to this as exegesis. Exegesis is when people analyze the scriptures to find out the original meaning. You ask yourself: What did the author of this text want the original audience to understand? This is the part of the journal entry where you will start to gather research and data to find God's original meaning in this section of the Bible. Allow the following questions to help you interpret the text.

History/Background of the Text
1. Who is the author of the book that you read? Research history and facts about the author of the book.
2. Who was the author's audience at the time?
3. When was the book written?
4. What were the **customs and culture** of this time?
5. Which **king ruled at the time**? What ordinances did this king create?
6. What was the significance of this governmental order? How did it impact society?

7. Do some research on the **setting**. What did you **learn about the geography of the setting?**
8. **Cross-reference**: What other scriptures relate to the scripture that you read? If you are reading the Old Testament, search for the New Testament scriptures that align with the Old Testament.
9. **Cross-reference themes**: Is this theme of the text repeated in different sections in the Bible?

Atmosphere
1. What is the theme of this chapter?
2. What is the **mood** of the chapter?
3. What is the **tone of voice the author uses to describe events?**
4. **What do you learn about God in this chapter?**
5. **What do you learn about the Holy Spirit?**
6. **What do you learn about Jesus?**

Words
1. Look up words that stand out to you (even if it is a simple word).
2. Look up words that you do not know.
3. Look up words that are specific to the **culture** of that book.
4. If you are reading the New Testament, look up words in the **Greek** language.
5. When reading the Old Testament, look up words in the **Hebrew** language.

Commentaries/Research Interpretation
If you are having a difficult time finding the interpretation, look up commentaries **AFTER you have done your due diligence to find the meaning of the scriptures. You can search the internet for commentaries. Compare about 2-3 commentaries to read what information is similar or different. When you compare commentaries, ask the Holy Spirit to lead you to the truth. (There will be some commentaries that are not biblical. If you find discrepancies in a

commentary, make sure that you have a scripture reference to justify why a point may be erroneous.)

3. General Application
The third step to studying the Bible is understanding how it can be applied to people's lives to live like Jesus. In this section, you will answer the following questions.

1. What is the universal lesson that these scriptures teach Christians?
2. What is a Christian principle (truth/idea) that you learned from these scriptures that can be applied to all Christians regardless of their denomination? For example- Jesus is the only way to be in a right relationship with God.
3. What does this scripture or passage help people understand in regards to their purpose, identity, and destiny?

4. Personal Application:
The third step to studying the Bible is identifying the personal application of the scriptures for your own life. Ask yourself these questions.
1. How can this scripture be applied to my personal life right now?
2. How do these scriptures personally affect me right now?
3. What is God trying to show me about myself, family, career, destiny, identity, ministry, current issues, etc?

Ultimately in this section, you will describe what God is trying to teach you through this study. Make this section personal. It may not be a message for everybody, but it is true for where God is taking you in life.

5. Action Steps
After you have observed and interpreted the scriptures, God wants you to take action. It is important to not only be a hearer of the Word but to be a doer of what He delineates for you in the Scriptures.

Write 2-3 next steps that God wants you to walk in after doing this study. Be specific.

6. Prayers Concerning the Scriptures

Before you close out your Bible study time, pray about what God is showing you about God, Jesus, and the Holy Spirit. Pray about how He is going to shape your view of Him and how you see yourself. What new confessions, declarations, or affirmations do you need to make so that God can help transform you?

Reminder: While completing the journal, refer back to these pages to read the full description for each section.

Websites to Visit: If you are starting on your journey of growing deeper in the Word, choose at least two-three reliable websites to use while you are studying. Have them bookmarked on your desktop. Here is a list of some suggestions.
o biblestudytools.com
o biblehub.com [Look up Greek and Hebrew here.]
o blueletterbible.org
o jewishencyclopedia.com [Learn more about Jewish history and culture here.]
o britannica.com
o encyclopedia.com

Journal Entry 1   DATE _____

SCRIPTURES FOR THE DAY

_____

_____

What version of the Bible are you reading?

_____

Does your version of the Bible list out a title for the section you chose to read? Write it out.

_____

_____

FOCUS: Research Question or Topic of Choice

_____

_____

1. Observations → Jeremiah, What Do You See?

Directions: After reading the scriptures for the day, write out 10 or more sentences about what you observed about these scriptures. During this time, <u>try to include two questions to ask God.</u> **Refer back to page 12 to see what you should include in the observations section.

1. What do you notice at first glance about the section you are reading?
2. What names were introduced?
3. What do you notice about the setting?
4. What words are repeated?
5. What words stood out to you?

2. Interpretation → Rightly Divide the Word of Truth.

Directions: It is time for you to do research. Dig deep and research the original meaning of the text.

Write at least a 10 sentence interpretation of what you read. Include in your answer what you learned about God, the Holy Spirit, and Jesus! Use your Bible study questions to write out the interpretation. Find articles, online sources, books, and other resources to help you answer questions. **Refer back to page 13 for the full list of information to help you interpret the text.**

While looking for the interpretation, think about the following questions.
History
1. Who wrote the book that you read?
2. What did you learn about the author?
3. Who was the author speaking to in the text?
4. Research some history about the author of the book.
5. What were the **customs and culture** of this time?
6. Which **king was in rule at the time**? What rulings did this king have?
7. Do some research on the **setting**. What did you **learn about the geography of the setting**?
8. **Cross-reference**: What other scriptures relate to the scripture that you read?

Words
1. Look up words that stand out to you, even if it is a simple word.
2. Look up words that you do not know.

Include in your answer:
1. What do you learn about God in this chapter?
2. What do you learn about the Holy Spirit?
3. What do you learn about Jesus?

Write out **the interpretation of the section of this text here.**

3. General Application → Be a Doer.

General Application: Ask yourself how these scriptures can be applied to the daily life of a Christian.

1. What is the universal lesson that these scriptures teach Christians?
2. What is a Christian principle (truth/idea) that you learned from these scriptures that can be applied to all Christians regardless of their denomination? For example- Jesus is the only way to be in a right relationship with God.
3. What does this scripture or passage help people understand in regards to their purpose, identity, and destiny?

Challenge yourself **to write out at least six sentences or more about how this scripture can be applied to the daily life of a Believer in Christ.**

4. Personal Application →
Take the Plank Out of Your Eye.

Personal Application: Describe what God is trying to teach you through this study.

Ask yourself:
1. How can this scripture be applied to my personal life right now?
2. How do these scriptures personally affect me right now?
3. What is God trying to show me about myself, family, career, destiny, identity, ministry, current issues, etc?

Challenge yourself **to write out six sentences or more.**

5. Action Steps → Faith Without Works is DEAD.

Directions: Write 2-3 next steps that God wants you to take after completing this study. Be specific.

Example: I need to delete my Instagram page <u>because</u> God revealed it is causing me to grumble and complain about my own life. Philippians 2:14 states, "Do everything without grumbling or arguing."

	Action Steps	**Why?**
1		
2		
3		

6. Prayer → Confess With Your Mouth.

Directions: In this section, you will write out a prayer concerning what God has shown you through the scriptures. Pray about what God is revealing to you about God, Jesus, and the Holy Spirit. Write out a prayer on how He is going to shape your view of Him and how you see yourself.

Write out new biblical declarations or life affirmations that you need to make so that God can help transform you.

Examples: (Based on Psalm 139:14) I declare that I am fearfully and wonderfully made. God help me to believe that You have a great and wonderful purpose for my life.

Let us Pray. Journal Below

Journal Entry 2 DATE _____

SCRIPTURES FOR THE DAY

_____

_____

What version of the Bible are you reading?

_____

Does your version of the Bible list out a title for the section you chose to read? Write it out.

_____

_____

FOCUS: Research Question or Topic of Choice

_____

_____

1. Observations → Jeremiah, What Do You See?

Directions: After reading the scriptures for the day, write out 10 or more sentences about what you observed about these scriptures. During this time, <u>try to include two questions to ask God.</u> **Refer back to page 12 to see what you should include in the observations section.

1. What do you notice at first glance about the section you are reading?
2. What names were introduced?
3. What do you notice about the setting?
4. What words are repeated?
5. What words stood out to you?

2. Interpretation → Rightly Divide the Word of Truth.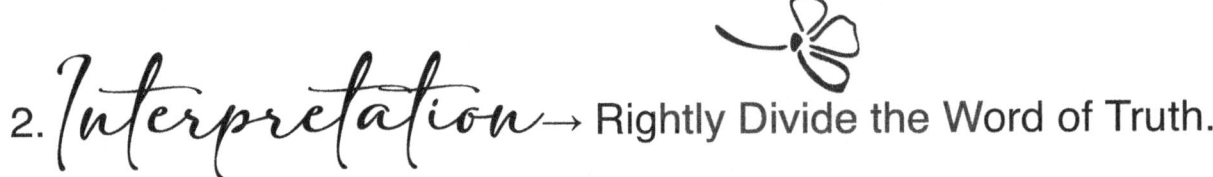

Directions: It is time for you to do research. Dig deep and research the original meaning of the text.

Write at least a 10 sentence interpretation of what you read. Include in your answer what you learned about God, the Holy Spirit, and Jesus! Use your Bible study questions to write out the interpretation. Find articles, online sources, books, and other resources to help you answer questions. **Refer back to page 13 for the full list of information to help you interpret the text.**

While looking for the interpretation, think about the following questions.
History
1. Who wrote the book that you read?
2. What did you learn about the author?
3. Who was the author speaking to in the text?
4. Research some history about the author of the book.
5. What were the **customs and culture** of this time?
6. Which **king was in rule at the time**? What rulings did this king have?
7. Do some research on the **setting**. What did you **learn about the geography of the setting**?
8. **Cross-reference**: What other scriptures relate to the scripture that you read?

Words
1. Look up words that stand out to you, even if it is a simple word.
2. Look up words that you do not know.

Include in your answer:
1. What do you learn about God in this chapter?
2. What do you learn about the Holy Spirit?
3. What do you learn about Jesus?

Write out **the interpretation of the section of this text here.**

3. General Application → Be a Doer.

General Application: Ask yourself how these scriptures can be applied to the daily life of a Christian.

1. What is the universal lesson that these scriptures teach Christians?
2. What is a Christian principle (truth/idea) that you learned from these scriptures that can be applied to all Christians regardless of their denomination? For example- Jesus is the only way to be in a right relationship with God.
3. What does this scripture or passage help people understand in regards to their purpose, identity, and destiny?

Challenge yourself **to write out at least six sentences or more about how this scripture can be applied to the daily life of a Believer in Christ.**

4. Personal Application
Take the Plank Out of Your Eye.

Personal Application: Describe what God is trying to teach you through this study.

Ask yourself:
1. How can this scripture be applied to my personal life right now?
2. How do these scriptures personally affect me right now?
3. What is God trying to show me about myself, family, career, destiny, identity, ministry, current issues, etc?

Challenge yourself **to write out six sentences or more.**

5. Action Steps → Faith Without Works is DEAD.

Directions: Write 2-3 next steps that God wants you to take after completing this study. Be specific.

Example: I need to delete my Instagram page <u>because</u> God revealed it is causing me to grumble and complain about my own life. Philippians 2:14 states, "Do everything without grumbling or arguing."

	Action Steps	**Why?**
1		
2		
3		

6. Prayer → Confess With Your Mouth.

Directions: In this section, you will write out a prayer concerning what God has shown you through the scriptures. Pray about what God is revealing to you about God, Jesus, and the Holy Spirit. Write out a prayer on how He is going to shape your view of Him and how you see yourself.

Write out new biblical declarations or life affirmations that you need to make so that God can help transform you.

Examples: (Based on Psalm 139:14) I declare that I am fearfully and wonderfully made. God help me to believe that You have a great and wonderful purpose for my life.

Let us Pray. Journal Below

Journal Entry 3   DATE _____

SCRIPTURES FOR THE DAY

_____

_____

What version of the Bible are you reading?

_____

Does your version of the Bible list out a title for the section you chose to read? Write it out.

_____

_____

FOCUS: Research Question or Topic of Choice

_____

_____

1. Observations → Jeremiah, What Do You See?

Directions: After reading the scriptures for the day, write out 10 or more sentences about what you observed about these scriptures. During this time, <u>try to include two questions to ask God.</u> **Refer back to page 12 to see what you should include in the observations section.

1. What do you notice at first glance about the section you are reading?
2. What names were introduced?
3. What do you notice about the setting?
4. What words are repeated?
5. What words stood out to you?

2. Interpretation → Rightly Divide the Word of Truth.

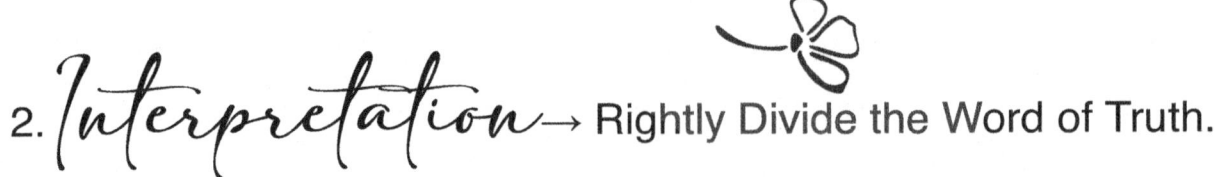

Directions: It is time for you to do research. Dig deep and research the original meaning of the text.

Write at least a 10 sentence interpretation of what you read. Include in your answer what you learned about God, the Holy Spirit, and Jesus! Use your Bible study questions to write out the interpretation. Find articles, online sources, books, and other resources to help you answer questions. **Refer back to page 13 for the full list of information to help you interpret the text.**

While looking for the interpretation, think about the following questions.
History
1. Who wrote the book that you read?
2. What did you learn about the author?
3. Who was the author speaking to in the text?
4. Research some history about the author of the book.
5. What were the **customs and culture** of this time?
6. Which **king was in rule at the time**? What rulings did this king have?
7. Do some research on the **setting**. What did you **learn about the geography of the setting**?
8. **Cross-reference**: What other scriptures relate to the scripture that you read?

Words
1. Look up words that stand out to you, even if it is a simple word.
2. Look up words that you do not know.

Include in your answer:
1. What do you learn about God in this chapter?
2. What do you learn about the Holy Spirit?
3. What do you learn about Jesus?

Write out **the interpretation of the section of this text here.**

3. General Application → Be a Doer.

General Application: Ask yourself how these scriptures can be applied to the daily life of a Christian.

1. What is the universal lesson that these scriptures teach Christians?
2. What is a Christian principle (truth/idea) that you learned from these scriptures that can be applied to all Christians regardless of their denomination? For example- Jesus is the only way to be in a right relationship with God.
3. What does this scripture or passage help people understand in regards to their purpose, identity, and destiny?

Challenge yourself to write out at least six sentences or more about how this scripture can be applied to the daily life of a Believer in Christ.

4. Personal Application
Take the Plank Out of Your Eye.

Personal Application: Describe what God is trying to teach you through this study.

Ask yourself:
1. How can this scripture be applied to my personal life right now?
2. How do these scriptures personally affect me right now?
3. What is God trying to show me about myself, family, career, destiny, identity, ministry, current issues, etc?

Challenge yourself **to write out six sentences or more.**

5. Action Steps → Faith Without Works is DEAD.

Directions: Write 2-3 next steps that God wants you to take after completing this study. Be specific.

Example: I need to delete my Instagram page <u>because</u> God revealed it is causing me to grumble and complain about my own life. Philippians 2:14 states, "Do everything without grumbling or arguing."

	Action Steps	Why?
1		
2		
3		

6. Prayer → Confess With Your Mouth.

Directions: In this section, you will write out a prayer concerning what God has shown you through the scriptures. Pray about what God is revealing to you about God, Jesus, and the Holy Spirit. Write out a prayer on how He is going to shape your view of Him and how you see yourself.

Write out new biblical declarations or life affirmations that you need to make so that God can help transform you.

Examples: (Based on Psalm 139:14) I declare that I am fearfully and wonderfully made. God help me to believe that You have a great and wonderful purpose for my life.

Let us Pray. Journal Below

Journal Entry 4　　　DATE _____

SCRIPTURES FOR THE DAY

_____

_____

What version of the Bible are you reading?

_____

Does your version of the Bible list out a title for the section you chose to read? Write it out.

_____

_____

FOCUS: Research Question or Topic of Choice

_____

_____

1. Observations → Jeremiah, What Do You See?

Directions: After reading the scriptures for the day, write out 10 or more sentences about what you observed about these scriptures. During this time, <u>try to include two questions to ask God.</u> **Refer back to page 12 to see what you should include in the observations section.

1. What do you notice at first glance about the section you are reading?
2. What names were introduced?
3. What do you notice about the setting?
4. What words are repeated?
5. What words stood out to you?

2. *Interpretation* → Rightly Divide the Word of Truth.

Directions: It is time for you to do research. Dig deep and research the original meaning of the text.

Write at least a 10 sentence interpretation of what you read. Include in your answer what you learned about God, the Holy Spirit, and Jesus! Use your Bible study questions to write out the interpretation. Find articles, online sources, books, and other resources to help you answer questions. **Refer back to page 13 for the full list of information to help you interpret the text.**

While looking for the interpretation, think about the following questions.
History
1. Who wrote the book that you read?
2. What did you learn about the author?
3. Who was the author speaking to in the text?
4. Research some history about the author of the book.
5. What were the **customs and culture** of this time?
6. Which **king was in rule at the time**? What rulings did this king have?
7. Do some research on the **setting**. What did you **learn about the geography of the setting**?
8. **Cross-reference**: What other scriptures relate to the scripture that you read?

Words
1. Look up words that stand out to you, even if it is a simple word.
2. Look up words that you do not know.

Include in your answer:
1. What do you learn about God in this chapter?
2. What do you learn about the Holy Spirit?
3. What do you learn about Jesus?

Write out **the interpretation of the section of this text here.**

3. General Application → Be a Doer.

General Application: Ask yourself how these scriptures can be applied to the daily life of a Christian.
1. What is the universal lesson that these scriptures teach Christians?
2. What is a Christian principle (truth/idea) that you learned from these scriptures that can be applied to all Christians regardless of their denomination? For example- Jesus is the only way to be in a right relationship with God.
3. What does this scripture or passage help people understand in regards to their purpose, identity, and destiny?

Challenge yourself to write out at least six sentences or more about how this scripture can be applied to the daily life of a Believer in Christ.

4. Personal Application
Take the Plank Out of Your Eye.

Personal Application: Describe what God is trying to teach you through this study.

Ask yourself:
1. How can this scripture be applied to my personal life right now?
2. How do these scriptures personally affect me right now?
3. What is God trying to show me about myself, family, career, destiny, identity, ministry, current issues, etc?

Challenge yourself **to write out six sentences or more.**

5. Action Steps → Faith Without Works is DEAD.

Directions: Write 2-3 next steps that God wants you to take after completing this study. Be specific.

Example: I need to delete my Instagram page <u>because</u> God revealed it is causing me to grumble and complain about my own life. Philippians 2:14 states, "Do everything without grumbling or arguing."

	Action Steps	**Why?**
1		
2		
3		

6. Prayer → Confess With Your Mouth.

Directions: In this section, you will write out a prayer concerning what God has shown you through the scriptures. Pray about what God is revealing to you about God, Jesus, and the Holy Spirit. Write out a prayer on how He is going to shape your view of Him and how you see yourself.

Write out new biblical declarations or life affirmations that you need to make so that God can help transform you.

Examples: (Based on Psalm 139:14) I declare that I am fearfully and wonderfully made. God help me to believe that You have a great and wonderful purpose for my life.

Let us Pray. Journal Below

Journal Entry 5

DATE _____

SCRIPTURES FOR THE DAY

_____

_____

What version of the Bible are you reading?

_____

Does your version of the Bible list out a title for the section you chose to read? Write it out.

_____

_____

FOCUS: Research Question or Topic of Choice

_____

_____

1. Observations → Jeremiah, What Do You See?

Directions: After reading the scriptures for the day, write out 10 or more sentences about what you observed about these scriptures. During this time, <u>try to include two questions to ask God.</u> **Refer back to page 12 to see what you should include in the observations section.

1. What do you notice at first glance about the section you are reading?
2. What names were introduced?
3. What do you notice about the setting?
4. What words are repeated?
5. What words stood out to you?

2. Interpretation → Rightly Divide the Word of Truth.

Directions: It is time for you to do research. Dig deep and research the original meaning of the text.

Write at least a 10 sentence interpretation of what you read. Include in your answer what you learned about God, the Holy Spirit, and Jesus! Use your Bible study questions to write out the interpretation. Find articles, online sources, books, and other resources to help you answer questions. **Refer back to page 13 for the full list of information to help you interpret the text.**

While looking for the interpretation, think about the following questions.
History
1. Who wrote the book that you read?
2. What did you learn about the author?
3. Who was the author speaking to in the text?
4. Research some history about the author of the book.
5. What were the **customs and culture** of this time?
6. Which **king was in rule at the time**? What rulings did this king have?
7. Do some research on the **setting**. What did you **learn about the geography of the setting**?
8. **Cross-reference**: What other scriptures relate to the scripture that you read?

Words
1. Look up words that stand out to you, even if it is a simple word.
2. Look up words that you do not know.

Include in your answer:
1. What do you learn about God in this chapter?
2. What do you learn about the Holy Spirit?
3. What do you learn about Jesus?

Write out the interpretation of the section of this text here.

3. General Application → Be a Doer.

General Application: Ask yourself how these scriptures can be applied to the daily life of a Christian.

1. What is the universal lesson that these scriptures teach Christians?
2. What is a Christian principle (truth/idea) that you learned from these scriptures that can be applied to all Christians regardless of their denomination? For example- Jesus is the only way to be in a right relationship with God.
3. What does this scripture or passage help people understand in regards to their purpose, identity, and destiny?

Challenge yourself **to write out at least six sentences or more about how this scripture can be applied to the daily life of a Believer in Christ.**

4. Personal Application
Take the Plank Out of Your Eye.

Personal Application: Describe what God is trying to teach you through this study.

Ask yourself:
1. How can this scripture be applied to my personal life right now?
2. How do these scriptures personally affect me right now?
3. What is God trying to show me about myself, family, career, destiny, identity, ministry, current issues, etc?

Challenge yourself **to write out six sentences or more.**

5. Action Steps → Faith Without Works is DEAD.

Directions: Write 2-3 next steps that God wants you to take after completing this study. Be specific.

Example: I need to delete my Instagram page <u>because</u> God revealed it is causing me to grumble and complain about my own life. Philippians 2:14 states, "Do everything without grumbling or arguing."

	Action Steps	Why?
1		
2		
3		

6. Prayer → Confess With Your Mouth.

Directions: In this section, you will write out a prayer concerning what God has shown you through the scriptures. Pray about what God is revealing to you about God, Jesus, and the Holy Spirit. Write out a prayer on how He is going to shape your view of Him and how you see yourself.

Write out new biblical declarations or life affirmations that you need to make so that God can help transform you.

Examples: (Based on Psalm 139:14) I declare that I am fearfully and wonderfully made. God help me to believe that You have a great and wonderful purpose for my life.

Let us Pray. Journal Below

Journal Entry 6   DATE _____

SCRIPTURES FOR THE DAY

_____

_____

What version of the Bible are you reading?

_____

Does your version of the Bible list out a title for the section you chose to read? Write it out.

_____

_____

FOCUS: Research Question or Topic of Choice

_____

_____

1. Observations → Jeremiah, What Do You See?

Directions: After reading the scriptures for the day, write out 10 or more sentences about what you observed about these scriptures. During this time, <u>try to include two questions to ask God.</u> **Refer back to page 12 to see what you should include in the observations section.
1. What do you notice at first glance about the section you are reading?
2. What names were introduced?
3. What do you notice about the setting?
4. What words are repeated?
5. What words stood out to you?

2. Interpretation → Rightly Divide the Word of Truth.

Directions: It is time for you to do research. Dig deep and research the original meaning of the text.

Write at least a 10 sentence interpretation of what you read. Include in your answer what you learned about God, the Holy Spirit, and Jesus! Use your Bible study questions to write out the interpretation. Find articles, online sources, books, and other resources to help you answer questions. **Refer back to page 13 for the full list of information to help you interpret the text.**

While looking for the interpretation, think about the following questions.
History
1. Who wrote the book that you read?
2. What did you learn about the author?
3. Who was the author speaking to in the text?
4. Research some history about the author of the book.
5. What were the **customs and culture** of this time?
6. Which **king was in rule at the time**? What rulings did this king have?
7. Do some research on the **setting**. What did you **learn about the geography of the setting**?
8. **Cross-reference**: What other scriptures relate to the scripture that you read?

Words
1. Look up words that stand out to you, even if it is a simple word.
2. Look up words that you do not know.

Include in your answer:
1. What do you learn about God in this chapter?
2. What do you learn about the Holy Spirit?
3. What do you learn about Jesus?

Write out the interpretation of the section of this text here.

3. General Application → Be a Doer.

General Application: Ask yourself how these scriptures can be applied to the daily life of a Christian.
1. What is the universal lesson that these scriptures teach Christians?
2. What is a Christian principle (truth/idea) that you learned from these scriptures that can be applied to all Christians regardless of their denomination? For example- Jesus is the only way to be in a right relationship with God.
3. What does this scripture or passage help people understand in regards to their purpose, identity, and destiny?

Challenge yourself **to write out at least six sentences or more about how this scripture can be applied to the daily life of a Believer in Christ.**

4. Personal Application
Take the Plank Out of Your Eye.

Personal Application: Describe what God is trying to teach you through this study.

Ask yourself:
1. How can this scripture be applied to my personal life right now?
2. How do these scriptures personally affect me right now?
3. What is God trying to show me about myself, family, career, destiny, identity, ministry, current issues, etc?

Challenge yourself **to write out six sentences or more.**

5. Action Steps → Faith Without Works is DEAD.

Directions: Write 2-3 next steps that God wants you to take after completing this study. Be specific.

Example: I need to delete my Instagram page <u>because</u> God revealed it is causing me to grumble and complain about my own life. Philippians 2:14 states, "Do everything without grumbling or arguing."

	Action Steps	Why?
1		
2		
3		

6. Prayer → Confess With Your Mouth.

Directions: In this section, you will write out a prayer concerning what God has shown you through the scriptures. Pray about what God is revealing to you about God, Jesus, and the Holy Spirit. Write out a prayer on how He is going to shape your view of Him and how you see yourself.

Write out new biblical declarations or life affirmations that you need to make so that God can help transform you.

Examples: (Based on Psalm 139:14) I declare that I am fearfully and wonderfully made. God help me to believe that You have a great and wonderful purpose for my life.

Let us Pray. Journal Below

Journal Entry 7

DATE _____

SCRIPTURES FOR THE DAY

_____

_____

What version of the Bible are you reading?

_____

Does your version of the Bible list out a title for the section you chose to read? Write it out.

_____

_____

FOCUS: Research Question or Topic of Choice

_____

_____

1. Observations → Jeremiah, What Do You See?

Directions: After reading the scriptures for the day, write out 10 or more sentences about what you observed about these scriptures. During this time, <u>try to include two questions to ask God.</u> **Refer back to page 12 to see what you should include in the observations section.

1. What do you notice at first glance about the section you are reading?
2. What names were introduced?
3. What do you notice about the setting?
4. What words are repeated?
5. What words stood out to you?

2. Interpretation → Rightly Divide the Word of Truth.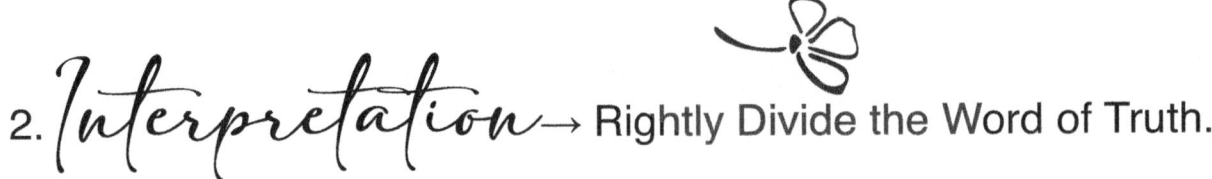

Directions: It is time for you to do research. Dig deep and research the original meaning of the text.

Write at least a 10 sentence interpretation of what you read. Include in your answer what you learned about God, the Holy Spirit, and Jesus! Use your Bible study questions to write out the interpretation. Find articles, online sources, books, and other resources to help you answer questions. **Refer back to page 13 for the full list of information to help you interpret the text.**

While looking for the interpretation, think about the following questions.
History
1. Who wrote the book that you read?
2. What did you learn about the author?
3. Who was the author speaking to in the text?
4. Research some history about the author of the book.
5. What were the **customs and culture** of this time?
6. Which **king was in rule at the time**? What rulings did this king have?
7. Do some research on the **setting**. What did you **learn about the geography of the setting**?
8. **Cross-reference**: What other scriptures relate to the scripture that you read?

Words
1. Look up words that stand out to you, even if it is a simple word.
2. Look up words that you do not know.

Include in your answer:
1. What do you learn about God in this chapter?
2. What do you learn about the Holy Spirit?
3. What do you learn about Jesus?

Write out **the interpretation of the section of this text here.**

3. General Application → Be a Doer.

General Application: Ask yourself how these scriptures can be applied to the daily life of a Christian.
1. What is the universal lesson that these scriptures teach Christians?
2. What is a Christian principle (truth/idea) that you learned from these scriptures that can be applied to all Christians regardless of their denomination? For example- Jesus is the only way to be in a right relationship with God.
3. What does this scripture or passage help people understand in regards to their purpose, identity, and destiny?

Challenge yourself to write out at least six sentences or more about how this scripture can be applied to the daily life of a Believer in Christ.

4. Personal Application →
Take the Plank Out of Your Eye.

Personal Application: Describe what God is trying to teach you through this study.

Ask yourself:
1. How can this scripture be applied to my personal life right now?
2. How do these scriptures personally affect me right now?
3. What is God trying to show me about myself, family, career, destiny, identity, ministry, current issues, etc?

Challenge yourself **to write out six sentences or more.**

5. Action Steps → Faith Without Works is DEAD.

Directions: Write 2-3 next steps that God wants you to take after completing this study. Be specific.

Example: I need to delete my Instagram page <u>because</u> God revealed it is causing me to grumble and complain about my own life. Philippians 2:14 states, "Do everything without grumbling or arguing."

	Action Steps	**Why?**
1		
2		
3		

6. Prayer → Confess With Your Mouth.

Directions: In this section, you will write out a prayer concerning what God has shown you through the scriptures. Pray about what God is revealing to you about God, Jesus, and the Holy Spirit. Write out a prayer on how He is going to shape your view of Him and how you see yourself.

Write out new biblical declarations or life affirmations that you need to make so that God can help transform you.

Examples: (Based on Psalm 139:14) I declare that I am fearfully and wonderfully made. God help me to believe that You have a great and wonderful purpose for my life.

Let us Pray. Journal Below

Journal Entry 8   DATE _____

SCRIPTURES FOR THE DAY

_____

_____

What version of the Bible are you reading?

_____

Does your version of the Bible list out a title for the section you chose to read? Write it out.

_____

_____

FOCUS: Research Question or Topic of Choice

_____

_____

1. Observations → Jeremiah, What Do You See?

Directions: After reading the scriptures for the day, write out 10 or more sentences about what you observed about these scriptures. During this time, <u>try to include two questions to ask God.</u> **Refer back to page 12 to see what you should include in the observations section.

1. What do you notice at first glance about the section you are reading?
2. What names were introduced?
3. What do you notice about the setting?
4. What words are repeated?
5. What words stood out to you?

2. *Interpretation* → Rightly Divide the Word of Truth.

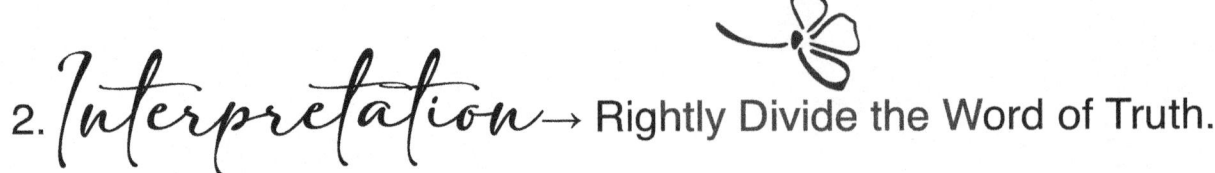

Directions: It is time for you to do research. Dig deep and research the original meaning of the text.

Write at least a 10 sentence interpretation of what you read. Include in your answer what you learned about God, the Holy Spirit, and Jesus! Use your Bible study questions to write out the interpretation. Find articles, online sources, books, and other resources to help you answer questions. **Refer back to page 13 for the full list of information to help you interpret the text.**

While looking for the interpretation, think about the following questions.
History
1. Who wrote the book that you read?
2. What did you learn about the author?
3. Who was the author speaking to in the text?
4. Research some history about the author of the book.
5. What were the **customs and culture** of this time?
6. Which **king was in rule at the time**? What rulings did this king have?
7. Do some research on the **setting**. What did you **learn about the geography of the setting**?
8. **Cross-reference**: What other scriptures relate to the scripture that you read?

Words
1. Look up words that stand out to you, even if it is a simple word.
2. Look up words that you do not know.

Include in your answer:
1. What do you learn about God in this chapter?
2. What do you learn about the Holy Spirit?
3. What do you learn about Jesus?

Write out **the interpretation of the section of this text here.**

3. General Application → Be a Doer.

General Application: Ask yourself how these scriptures can be applied to the daily life of a Christian.

1. What is the universal lesson that these scriptures teach Christians?
2. What is a Christian principle (truth/idea) that you learned from these scriptures that can be applied to all Christians regardless of their denomination? For example- Jesus is the only way to be in a right relationship with God.
3. What does this scripture or passage help people understand in regards to their purpose, identity, and destiny?

Challenge yourself to write out at least six sentences or more about how this scripture can be applied to the daily life of a Believer in Christ.

4. Personal Application →
Take the Plank Out of Your Eye.

Personal Application: Describe what God is trying to teach you through this study.

Ask yourself:
1. How can this scripture be applied to my personal life right now?
2. How do these scriptures personally affect me right now?
3. What is God trying to show me about myself, family, career, destiny, identity, ministry, current issues, etc?

Challenge yourself **to write out six sentences or more.**

5. Action Steps → Faith Without Works is DEAD.

Directions: Write 2-3 next steps that God wants you to take after completing this study. Be specific.

Example: I need to delete my Instagram page <u>because</u> God revealed it is causing me to grumble and complain about my own life. Philippians 2:14 states, "Do everything without grumbling or arguing."

	Action Steps	**Why?**
1		
2		
3		

6. *Prayer* → Confess With Your Mouth.

Directions: In this section, you will write out a prayer concerning what God has shown you through the scriptures. Pray about what God is revealing to you about God, Jesus, and the Holy Spirit. Write out a prayer on how He is going to shape your view of Him and how you see yourself.

Write out new biblical declarations or life affirmations that you need to make so that God can help transform you.

Examples: (Based on Psalm 139:14) I declare that I am fearfully and wonderfully made. God help me to believe that You have a great and wonderful purpose for my life.

Let us Pray. Journal Below

Journal Entry 9   DATE _____

SCRIPTURES FOR THE DAY

_____

_____

What version of the Bible are you reading?

_____

Does your version of the Bible list out a title for the section you chose to read? Write it out.

_____

_____

FOCUS: Research Question or Topic of Choice

_____

_____

1. Observations → Jeremiah, What Do You See?

Directions: After reading the scriptures for the day, write out 10 or more sentences about what you observed about these scriptures. During this time, <u>try to include two questions to ask God.</u> **Refer back to page 12 to see what you should include in the observations section.

1. What do you notice at first glance about the section you are reading?
2. What names were introduced?
3. What do you notice about the setting?
4. What words are repeated?
5. What words stood out to you?

2. *Interpretation* → Rightly Divide the Word of Truth.

Directions: It is time for you to do research. Dig deep and research the original meaning of the text.

Write at least a 10 sentence interpretation of what you read. Include in your answer what you learned about God, the Holy Spirit, and Jesus! Use your Bible study questions to write out the interpretation. Find articles, online sources, books, and other resources to help you answer questions. **Refer back to page 13 for the full list of information to help you interpret the text.**

While looking for the interpretation, think about the following questions.
History
1. Who wrote the book that you read?
2. What did you learn about the author?
3. Who was the author speaking to in the text?
4. Research some history about the author of the book.
5. What were the **customs and culture** of this time?
6. Which **king was in rule at the time**? What rulings did this king have?
7. Do some research on the **setting**. What did you **learn about the geography of the setting**?
8. **Cross-reference**: What other scriptures relate to the scripture that you read?

Words
1. Look up words that stand out to you, even if it is a simple word.
2. Look up words that you do not know.

Include in your answer:
1. What do you learn about God in this chapter?
2. What do you learn about the Holy Spirit?
3. What do you learn about Jesus?

Write out the interpretation of the section of this text here.

3. General Application → Be a Doer.

General Application: Ask yourself how these scriptures can be applied to the daily life of a Christian.
1. What is the universal lesson that these scriptures teach Christians?
2. What is a Christian principle (truth/idea) that you learned from these scriptures that can be applied to all Christians regardless of their denomination? For example- Jesus is the only way to be in a right relationship with God.
3. What does this scripture or passage help people understand in regards to their purpose, identity, and destiny?

Challenge yourself **to write out at least six sentences or more about how this scripture can be applied to the daily life of a Believer in Christ.**

4. Personal Application →

Take the Plank Out of Your Eye.

Personal Application: Describe what God is trying to teach you through this study.

Ask yourself:
1. How can this scripture be applied to my personal life right now?
2. How do these scriptures personally affect me right now?
3. What is God trying to show me about myself, family, career, destiny, identity, ministry, current issues, etc?

Challenge yourself **to write out six sentences or more.**

5. Action Steps → Faith Without Works is DEAD.

Directions: Write 2-3 next steps that God wants you to take after completing this study. Be specific.

Example: I need to delete my Instagram page <u>because</u> God revealed it is causing me to grumble and complain about my own life. Philippians 2:14 states, "Do everything without grumbling or arguing."

	Action Steps	Why?
1		
2		
3		

6. Prayer → Confess With Your Mouth.

Directions: In this section, you will write out a prayer concerning what God has shown you through the scriptures. Pray about what God is revealing to you about God, Jesus, and the Holy Spirit. Write out a prayer on how He is going to shape your view of Him and how you see yourself.

Write out new biblical declarations or life affirmations that you need to make so that God can help transform you.

Examples: (Based on Psalm 139:14) I declare that I am fearfully and wonderfully made. God help me to believe that You have a great and wonderful purpose for my life.

Let us Pray. Journal Below

Journal Entry 10   DATE _____

SCRIPTURES FOR THE DAY

_____

_____

What version of the Bible are you reading?

_____

Does your version of the Bible list out a title for the section you chose to read? Write it out.

_____

_____

FOCUS: Research Question or Topic of Choice

_____

_____

1. Observations → Jeremiah, What Do You See?

Directions: After reading the scriptures for the day, write out 10 or more sentences about what you observed about these scriptures. During this time, <u>try to include two questions to ask God.</u> **Refer back to page 12 to see what you should include in the observations section.

1. What do you notice at first glance about the section you are reading?
2. What names were introduced?
3. What do you notice about the setting?
4. What words are repeated?
5. What words stood out to you?

2. Interpretation → Rightly Divide the Word of Truth.

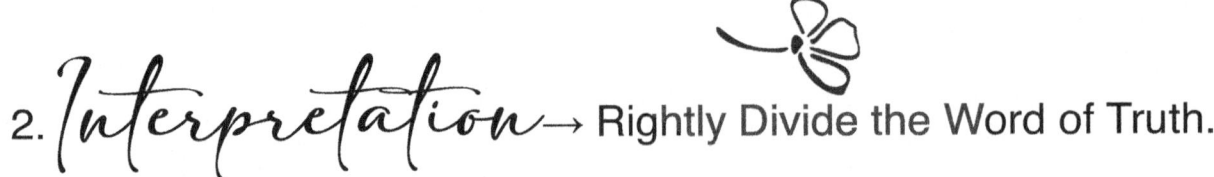

Directions: It is time for you to do research. Dig deep and research the original meaning of the text.

Write at least a 10 sentence interpretation of what you read. Include in your answer what you learned about God, the Holy Spirit, and Jesus! Use your Bible study questions to write out the interpretation. Find articles, online sources, books, and other resources to help you answer questions. **Refer back to page 13 for the full list of information to help you interpret the text.**

While looking for the interpretation, think about the following questions.
History
1. Who wrote the book that you read?
2. What did you learn about the author?
3. Who was the author speaking to in the text?
4. Research some history about the author of the book.
5. What were the **customs and culture** of this time?
6. Which **king was in rule at the time**? What rulings did this king have?
7. Do some research on the **setting**. What did you **learn about the geography of the setting**?
8. **Cross-reference**: What other scriptures relate to the scripture that you read?

Words
1. Look up words that stand out to you, even if it is a simple word.
2. Look up words that you do not know.

Include in your answer:
1. What do you learn about God in this chapter?
2. What do you learn about the Holy Spirit?
3. What do you learn about Jesus?

Write out the interpretation of the section of this text here.

3. General Application → Be a Doer.

General Application: Ask yourself how these scriptures can be applied to the daily life of a Christian.

1. What is the universal lesson that these scriptures teach Christians?
2. What is a Christian principle (truth/idea) that you learned from these scriptures that can be applied to all Christians regardless of their denomination? For example- Jesus is the only way to be in a right relationship with God.
3. What does this scripture or passage help people understand in regards to their purpose, identity, and destiny?

Challenge yourself **to write out at least six sentences or more about how this scripture can be applied to the daily life of a Believer in Christ.**

4. Personal Application →
Take the Plank Out of Your Eye.

Personal Application: Describe what God is trying to teach you through this study.

Ask yourself:
1. How can this scripture be applied to my personal life right now?
2. How do these scriptures personally affect me right now?
3. What is God trying to show me about myself, family, career, destiny, identity, ministry, current issues, etc?

Challenge yourself **to write out six sentences or more.**

5. Action Steps → Faith Without Works is DEAD.

Directions: Write 2-3 next steps that God wants you to take after completing this study. Be specific.

Example: I need to delete my Instagram page <u>because</u> God revealed it is causing me to grumble and complain about my own life. Philippians 2:14 states, "Do everything without grumbling or arguing."

	Action Steps	Why?
1		
2		
3		

6. Prayer → Confess With Your Mouth.

Directions: In this section, you will write out a prayer concerning what God has shown you through the scriptures. Pray about what God is revealing to you about God, Jesus, and the Holy Spirit. Write out a prayer on how He is going to shape your view of Him and how you see yourself.

Write out new biblical declarations or life affirmations that you need to make so that God can help transform you.

Examples: (Based on Psalm 139:14) I declare that I am fearfully and wonderfully made. God help me to believe that You have a great and wonderful purpose for my life.

Let us Pray. Journal Below

Journal Entry 11   DATE

SCRIPTURES FOR THE DAY

_____

_____

What version of the Bible are you reading?

_____

Does your version of the Bible list out a title for the section you chose to read? Write it out.

_____

_____

FOCUS: Research Question or Topic of Choice

_____

_____

1. Observations → Jeremiah, What Do You See?

Directions: After reading the scriptures for the day, write out 10 or more sentences about what you observed about these scriptures. During this time, try to include two questions to ask God. **Refer back to page 12 to see what you should include in the observations section.
1. What do you notice at first glance about the section you are reading?
2. What names were introduced?
3. What do you notice about the setting?
4. What words are repeated?
5. What words stood out to you?

2. *Interpretation* → Rightly Divide the Word of Truth.

Directions: It is time for you to do research. Dig deep and research the original meaning of the text.

Write at least a 10 sentence interpretation of what you read. Include in your answer what you learned about God, the Holy Spirit, and Jesus! Use your Bible study questions to write out the interpretation. Find articles, online sources, books, and other resources to help you answer questions. **Refer back to page 13 for the full list of information to help you interpret the text.**

While looking for the interpretation, think about the following questions.
History
1. Who wrote the book that you read?
2. What did you learn about the author?
3. Who was the author speaking to in the text?
4. Research some history about the author of the book.
5. What were the **customs and culture** of this time?
6. Which **king was in rule at the time**? What rulings did this king have?
7. Do some research on the **setting**. What did you **learn about the geography of the setting**?
8. **Cross-reference**: What other scriptures relate to the scripture that you read?

Words
1. Look up words that stand out to you, even if it is a simple word.
2. Look up words that you do not know.

Include in your answer:
1. What do you learn about God in this chapter?
2. What do you learn about the Holy Spirit?
3. What do you learn about Jesus?

Write out the interpretation of the section of this text here.

3. General Application → Be a Doer.

General Application: Ask yourself how these scriptures can be applied to the daily life of a Christian.
1. What is the universal lesson that these scriptures teach Christians?
2. What is a Christian principle (truth/idea) that you learned from these scriptures that can be applied to all Christians regardless of their denomination? For example- Jesus is the only way to be in a right relationship with God.
3. What does this scripture or passage help people understand in regards to their purpose, identity, and destiny?

Challenge yourself **to write out at least six sentences or more about how this scripture can be applied to the daily life of a Believer in Christ.**

4. Personal Application
Take the Plank Out of Your Eye.

Personal Application: Describe what God is trying to teach you through this study.
Ask yourself:
1. How can this scripture be applied to my personal life right now?
2. How do these scriptures personally affect me right now?
3. What is God trying to show me about myself, family, career, destiny, identity, ministry, current issues, etc?

Challenge yourself **to write out six sentences or more.**

5. Action Steps → Faith Without Works is DEAD.

Directions: Write 2-3 next steps that God wants you to take after completing this study. Be specific.

Example: I need to delete my Instagram page <u>because</u> God revealed it is causing me to grumble and complain about my own life. Philippians 2:14 states, "Do everything without grumbling or arguing."

	Action Steps	Why?
1		
2		
3		

6. Prayer → Confess With Your Mouth.

Directions: In this section, you will write out a prayer concerning what God has shown you through the scriptures. Pray about what God is revealing to you about God, Jesus, and the Holy Spirit. Write out a prayer on how He is going to shape your view of Him and how you see yourself.

Write out new biblical declarations or life affirmations that you need to make so that God can help transform you.

Examples: (Based on Psalm 139:14) I declare that I am fearfully and wonderfully made. God help me to believe that You have a great and wonderful purpose for my life.

Let us Pray. Journal Below

Journal Entry 12

DATE _____

SCRIPTURES FOR THE DAY

_____

_____

What version of the Bible are you reading?

_____

Does your version of the Bible list out a title for the section you chose to read? Write it out.

_____

_____

FOCUS: Research Question or Topic of Choice

_____

_____

1. Observations → Jeremiah, What Do You See?

Directions: After reading the scriptures for the day, write out 10 or more sentences about what you observed about these scriptures. During this time, <u>try to include two questions to ask God.</u> **Refer back to page 12 to see what you should include in the observations section.

1. What do you notice at first glance about the section you are reading?
2. What names were introduced?
3. What do you notice about the setting?
4. What words are repeated?
5. What words stood out to you?

2. Interpretation → Rightly Divide the Word of Truth.

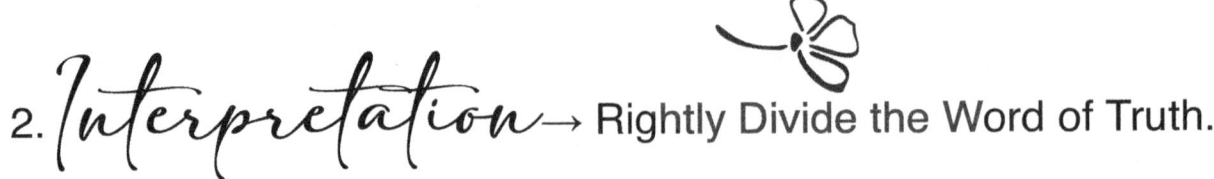

Directions: It is time for you to do research. Dig deep and research the original meaning of the text.

Write at least a 10 sentence interpretation of what you read. Include in your answer what you learned about God, the Holy Spirit, and Jesus! Use your Bible study questions to write out the interpretation. Find articles, online sources, books, and other resources to help you answer questions. **Refer back to page 13 for the full list of information to help you interpret the text.**

While looking for the interpretation, think about the following questions.
History
1. Who wrote the book that you read?
2. What did you learn about the author?
3. Who was the author speaking to in the text?
4. Research some history about the author of the book.
5. What were the **customs and culture** of this time?
6. Which **king was in rule at the time**? What rulings did this king have?
7. Do some research on the **setting**. What did you **learn about the geography of the setting**?
8. **Cross-reference**: What other scriptures relate to the scripture that you read?

Words
1. Look up words that stand out to you, even if it is a simple word.
2. Look up words that you do not know.

Include in your answer:
1. What do you learn about God in this chapter?
2. What do you learn about the Holy Spirit?
3. What do you learn about Jesus?

Write out the interpretation of the section of this text here.

3. General Application → Be a Doer.

General Application: Ask yourself how these scriptures can be applied to the daily life of a Christian.

1. What is the universal lesson that these scriptures teach Christians?
2. What is a Christian principle (truth/idea) that you learned from these scriptures that can be applied to all Christians regardless of their denomination? For example- Jesus is the only way to be in a right relationship with God.
3. What does this scripture or passage help people understand in regards to their purpose, identity, and destiny?

Challenge yourself **to write out at least six sentences or more about how this scripture can be applied to the daily life of a Believer in Christ.**

4. Personal Application
Take the Plank Out of Your Eye.

Personal Application: Describe what God is trying to teach you through this study.

Ask yourself:
1. How can this scripture be applied to my personal life right now?
2. How do these scriptures personally affect me right now?
3. What is God trying to show me about myself, family, career, destiny, identity, ministry, current issues, etc?

Challenge yourself **to write out six sentences or more.**

_____

_____

_____

_____

_____

_____

5. Action Steps → Faith Without Works is DEAD.

Directions: Write 2-3 next steps that God wants you to take after completing this study. Be specific.

Example: I need to delete my Instagram page <u>because</u> God revealed it is causing me to grumble and complain about my own life. Philippians 2:14 states, "Do everything without grumbling or arguing."

	Action Steps	Why?
1		
2		
3		

6. Prayer → Confess With Your Mouth.

Directions: In this section, you will write out a prayer concerning what God has shown you through the scriptures. Pray about what God is revealing to you about God, Jesus, and the Holy Spirit. Write out a prayer on how He is going to shape your view of Him and how you see yourself.

Write out new biblical declarations or life affirmations that you need to make so that God can help transform you.

Examples: (Based on Psalm 139:14) I declare that I am fearfully and wonderfully made. God help me to believe that You have a great and wonderful purpose for my life.

Let us Pray. Journal Below

Journal Entry 13

DATE _____

SCRIPTURES FOR THE DAY

_____

_____

What version of the Bible are you reading?

_____

Does your version of the Bible list out a title for the section you chose to read? Write it out.

_____

_____

FOCUS: Research Question or Topic of Choice

_____

_____

1. Observations → Jeremiah, What Do You See?

Directions: After reading the scriptures for the day, write out 10 or more sentences about what you observed about these scriptures. During this time, <u>try to include two questions to ask God.</u> **Refer back to page 12 to see what you should include in the observations section.

1. What do you notice at first glance about the section you are reading?
2. What names were introduced?
3. What do you notice about the setting?
4. What words are repeated?
5. What words stood out to you?

2. Interpretation → Rightly Divide the Word of Truth.

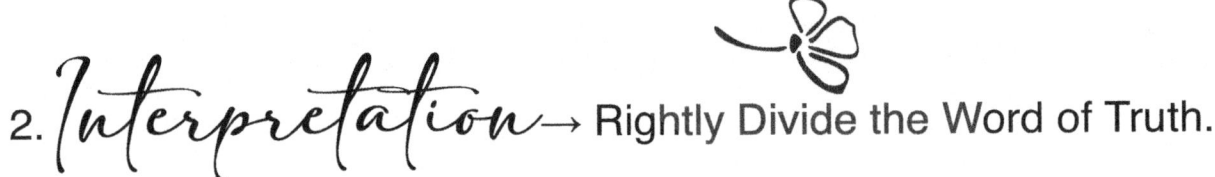

Directions: It is time for you to do research. Dig deep and research the original meaning of the text.

Write at least a 10 sentence interpretation of what you read. Include in your answer what you learned about God, the Holy Spirit, and Jesus! Use your Bible study questions to write out the interpretation. Find articles, online sources, books, and other resources to help you answer questions. **Refer back to page 13 for the full list of information to help you interpret the text.**

While looking for the interpretation, think about the following questions.
History
1. Who wrote the book that you read?
2. What did you learn about the author?
3. Who was the author speaking to in the text?
4. Research some history about the author of the book.
5. What were the **customs and culture** of this time?
6. Which **king was in rule at the time**? What rulings did this king have?
7. Do some research on the **setting**. What did you **learn about the geography of the setting**?
8. **Cross-reference**: What other scriptures relate to the scripture that you read?

Words
1. Look up words that stand out to you, even if it is a simple word.
2. Look up words that you do not know.

Include in your answer:
1. What do you learn about God in this chapter?
2. What do you learn about the Holy Spirit?
3. What do you learn about Jesus?

Write out the interpretation of the section of this text here.

3. General Application → Be a Doer.

General Application: Ask yourself how these scriptures can be applied to the daily life of a Christian.

1. What is the universal lesson that these scriptures teach Christians?
2. What is a Christian principle (truth/idea) that you learned from these scriptures that can be applied to all Christians regardless of their denomination? For example- Jesus is the only way to be in a right relationship with God.
3. What does this scripture or passage help people understand in regards to their purpose, identity, and destiny?

Challenge yourself to write out at least six sentences or more about how this scripture can be applied to the daily life of a Believer in Christ.

4. Personal Application
Take the Plank Out of Your Eye.

Personal Application: Describe what God is trying to teach you through this study.

Ask yourself:
1. How can this scripture be applied to my personal life right now?
2. How do these scriptures personally affect me right now?
3. What is God trying to show me about myself, family, career, destiny, identity, ministry, current issues, etc?

Challenge yourself **to write out six sentences or more.**

_____

_____

_____

_____

_____

_____

5. Action Steps → Faith Without Works is DEAD.

Directions: Write 2-3 next steps that God wants you to take after completing this study. Be specific.

Example: I need to delete my Instagram page <u>because</u> God revealed it is causing me to grumble and complain about my own life. Philippians 2:14 states, "Do everything without grumbling or arguing."

	Action Steps	Why?
1		
2		
3		

6. Prayer → Confess With Your Mouth.

Directions: In this section, you will write out a prayer concerning what God has shown you through the scriptures. Pray about what God is revealing to you about God, Jesus, and the Holy Spirit. Write out a prayer on how He is going to shape your view of Him and how you see yourself.

Write out new biblical declarations or life affirmations that you need to make so that God can help transform you.

Examples: (Based on Psalm 139:14) I declare that I am fearfully and wonderfully made. God help me to believe that You have a great and wonderful purpose for my life.

Let us Pray. Journal Below

Journal Entry 14   DATE _____

SCRIPTURES FOR THE DAY

_____

_____

What version of the Bible are you reading?

_____

Does your version of the Bible list out a title for the section you chose to read? Write it out.

_____

_____

FOCUS: Research Question or Topic of Choice

_____

_____

1.  Observations → Jeremiah, What Do You See?

Directions: After reading the scriptures for the day, write out 10 or more sentences about what you observed about these scriptures. During this time, try to include two questions to ask God. **Refer back to page 12 to see what you should include in the observations section.
1. What do you notice at first glance about the section you are reading?
2. What names were introduced?
3. What do you notice about the setting?
4. What words are repeated?
5. What words stood out to you?

2. *Interpretation* → Rightly Divide the Word of Truth.

Directions: It is time for you to do research. Dig deep and research the original meaning of the text.

Write at least a 10 sentence interpretation of what you read. Include in your answer what you learned about God, the Holy Spirit, and Jesus! Use your Bible study questions to write out the interpretation. Find articles, online sources, books, and other resources to help you answer questions. **Refer back to page 13 for the full list of information to help you interpret the text.**

While looking for the interpretation, think about the following questions.
History
1. Who wrote the book that you read?
2. What did you learn about the author?
3. Who was the author speaking to in the text?
4. Research some history about the author of the book.
5. What were the **customs and culture** of this time?
6. Which **king was in rule at the time**? What rulings did this king have?
7. Do some research on the **setting**. What did you **learn about the geography of the setting**?
8. **Cross-reference**: What other scriptures relate to the scripture that you read?

Words
1. Look up words that stand out to you, even if it is a simple word.
2. Look up words that you do not know.

Include in your answer:
1. What do you learn about God in this chapter?
2. What do you learn about the Holy Spirit?
3. What do you learn about Jesus?

Write out the interpretation of the section of this text here.

3. *General Application* → Be a Doer.

General Application: Ask yourself how these scriptures can be applied to the daily life of a Christian.
1. What is the universal lesson that these scriptures teach Christians?
2. What is a Christian principle (truth/idea) that you learned from these scriptures that can be applied to all Christians regardless of their denomination? For example- Jesus is the only way to be in a right relationship with God.
3. What does this scripture or passage help people understand in regards to their purpose, identity, and destiny?

Challenge yourself **to write out at least six sentences or more about how this scripture can be applied to the daily life of a Believer in Christ.**

4. Personal Application →
Take the Plank Out of Your Eye.

Personal Application: Describe what God is trying to teach you through this study.

Ask yourself:
1. How can this scripture be applied to my personal life right now?
2. How do these scriptures personally affect me right now?
3. What is God trying to show me about myself, family, career, destiny, identity, ministry, current issues, etc?

Challenge yourself **to write out six sentences or more.**

5. Action Steps → Faith Without Works is DEAD.

Directions: Write 2-3 next steps that God wants you to take after completing this study. Be specific.

Example: I need to delete my Instagram page <u>because</u> God revealed it is causing me to grumble and complain about my own life. Philippians 2:14 states, "Do everything without grumbling or arguing."

	Action Steps	**Why?**
1		
2		
3		

6. Prayer → Confess With Your Mouth.

Directions: In this section, you will write out a prayer concerning what God has shown you through the scriptures. Pray about what God is revealing to you about God, Jesus, and the Holy Spirit. Write out a prayer on how He is going to shape your view of Him and how you see yourself.

Write out new biblical declarations or life affirmations that you need to make so that God can help transform you.

Examples: (Based on Psalm 139:14) I declare that I am fearfully and wonderfully made. God help me to believe that You have a great and wonderful purpose for my life.

Let us Pray. Journal Below

Journal Entry 15

DATE _____

SCRIPTURES FOR THE DAY

_____

_____

What version of the Bible are you reading?

_____

Does your version of the Bible list out a title for the section you chose to read? Write it out.

_____

_____

FOCUS: Research Question or Topic of Choice

_____

_____

1. Observations → Jeremiah, What Do You See?

Directions: After reading the scriptures for the day, write out 10 or more sentences about what you observed about these scriptures. During this time, <u>try to include two questions to ask God.</u> **Refer back to page 12 to see what you should include in the observations section.

1. What do you notice at first glance about the section you are reading?
2. What names were introduced?
3. What do you notice about the setting?
4. What words are repeated?
5. What words stood out to you?

2. Interpretation → Rightly Divide the Word of Truth.

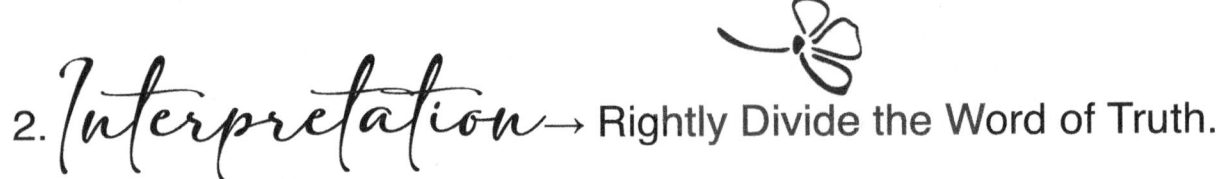

Directions: It is time for you to do research. Dig deep and research the original meaning of the text.

Write at least a 10 sentence interpretation of what you read. Include in your answer what you learned about God, the Holy Spirit, and Jesus! Use your Bible study questions to write out the interpretation. Find articles, online sources, books, and other resources to help you answer questions. **Refer back to page 13 for the full list of information to help you interpret the text.**

While looking for the interpretation, think about the following questions.
History
1. Who wrote the book that you read?
2. What did you learn about the author?
3. Who was the author speaking to in the text?
4. Research some history about the author of the book.
5. What were the **customs and culture** of this time?
6. Which **king was in rule at the time**? What rulings did this king have?
7. Do some research on the **setting**. What did you **learn about the geography of the setting**?
8. **Cross-reference**: What other scriptures relate to the scripture that you read?

Words
1. Look up words that stand out to you, even if it is a simple word.
2. Look up words that you do not know.

Include in your answer:
1. What do you learn about God in this chapter?
2. What do you learn about the Holy Spirit?
3. What do you learn about Jesus?

Write out the interpretation of the section of this text here.

3. General Application → Be a Doer.

General Application: Ask yourself how these scriptures can be applied to the daily life of a Christian.
1. What is the universal lesson that these scriptures teach Christians?
2. What is a Christian principle (truth/idea) that you learned from these scriptures that can be applied to all Christians regardless of their denomination? For example- Jesus is the only way to be in a right relationship with God.
3. What does this scripture or passage help people understand in regards to their purpose, identity, and destiny?

Challenge yourself to write out at least six sentences or more about how this scripture can be applied to the daily life of a Believer in Christ.

4. Personal Application
Take the Plank Out of Your Eye.

Personal Application: Describe what God is trying to teach you through this study.

Ask yourself:
1. How can this scripture be applied to my personal life right now?
2. How do these scriptures personally affect me right now?
3. What is God trying to show me about myself, family, career, destiny, identity, ministry, current issues, etc?

Challenge yourself **to write out six sentences or more.**

5. Action Steps → Faith Without Works is DEAD.

Directions: Write 2-3 next steps that God wants you to take after completing this study. Be specific.

Example: I need to delete my Instagram page <u>because</u> God revealed it is causing me to grumble and complain about my own life. Philippians 2:14 states, "Do everything without grumbling or arguing."

	Action Steps	**Why?**
1		
2		
3		

6. Prayer → Confess With Your Mouth.

Directions: In this section, you will write out a prayer concerning what God has shown you through the scriptures. Pray about what God is revealing to you about God, Jesus, and the Holy Spirit. Write out a prayer on how He is going to shape your view of Him and how you see yourself.

Write out new biblical declarations or life affirmations that you need to make so that God can help transform you.

Examples: (Based on Psalm 139:14) I declare that I am fearfully and wonderfully made. God help me to believe that You have a great and wonderful purpose for my life.

Let us Pray. Journal Below

Journal Entry 16 DATE _____

SCRIPTURES FOR THE DAY

_____

_____

What version of the Bible are you reading?

_____

Does your version of the Bible list out a title for the section you chose to read? Write it out.

_____

_____

FOCUS: Research Question or Topic of Choice

_____

_____

1.  Observations → Jeremiah, What Do You See?

Directions: After reading the scriptures for the day, write out 10 or more sentences about what you observed about these scriptures. During this time, <u>try to include two questions to ask God.</u> **Refer back to page 12 to see what you should include in the observations section.

1. What do you notice at first glance about the section you are reading?
2. What names were introduced?
3. What do you notice about the setting?
4. What words are repeated?
5. What words stood out to you?

2. Interpretation → Rightly Divide the Word of Truth.

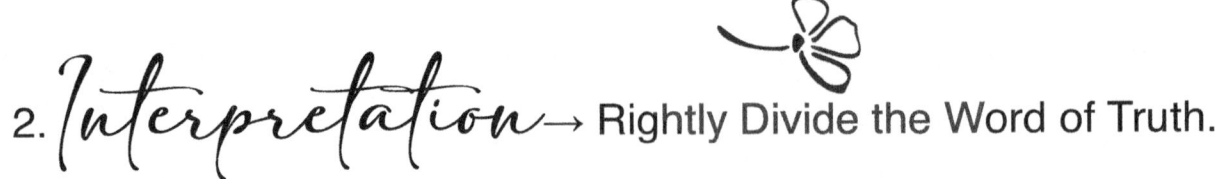

Directions: It is time for you to do research. Dig deep and research the original meaning of the text.

Write at least a 10 sentence interpretation of what you read. Include in your answer what you learned about God, the Holy Spirit, and Jesus! Use your Bible study questions to write out the interpretation. Find articles, online sources, books, and other resources to help you answer questions. **Refer back to page 13 for the full list of information to help you interpret the text.**

While looking for the interpretation, think about the following questions.
History
1. Who wrote the book that you read?
2. What did you learn about the author?
3. Who was the author speaking to in the text?
4. Research some history about the author of the book.
5. What were the **customs and culture** of this time?
6. Which **king was in rule at the time**? What rulings did this king have?
7. Do some research on the **setting**. What did you **learn about the geography of the setting**?
8. **Cross-reference**: What other scriptures relate to the scripture that you read?

Words
1. Look up words that stand out to you, even if it is a simple word.
2. Look up words that you do not know.

Include in your answer:
1. What do you learn about God in this chapter?
2. What do you learn about the Holy Spirit?
3. What do you learn about Jesus?

Write out the interpretation of the section of this text here.

3. General Application → Be a Doer.

General Application: Ask yourself how these scriptures can be applied to the daily life of a Christian.
1. What is the universal lesson that these scriptures teach Christians?
2. What is a Christian principle (truth/idea) that you learned from these scriptures that can be applied to all Christians regardless of their denomination? For example- Jesus is the only way to be in a right relationship with God.
3. What does this scripture or passage help people understand in regards to their purpose, identity, and destiny?

Challenge yourself to write out at least six sentences or more about how this scripture can be applied to the daily life of a Believer in Christ.

4. Personal Application
Take the Plank Out of Your Eye.

Personal Application: Describe what God is trying to teach you through this study.

Ask yourself:
1. How can this scripture be applied to my personal life right now?
2. How do these scriptures personally affect me right now?
3. What is God trying to show me about myself, family, career, destiny, identity, ministry, current issues, etc?

Challenge yourself **to write out six sentences or more.**

5. Action Steps → Faith Without Works is DEAD.

Directions: Write 2-3 next steps that God wants you to take after completing this study. Be specific.

Example: I need to delete my Instagram page <u>because</u> God revealed it is causing me to grumble and complain about my own life. Philippians 2:14 states, "Do everything without grumbling or arguing."

	Action Steps	**Why?**
1		
2		
3		

6. Prayer → Confess With Your Mouth.

Directions: In this section, you will write out a prayer concerning what God has shown you through the scriptures. Pray about what God is revealing to you about God, Jesus, and the Holy Spirit. Write out a prayer on how He is going to shape your view of Him and how you see yourself.

Write out new biblical declarations or life affirmations that you need to make so that God can help transform you.

Examples: (Based on Psalm 139:14) I declare that I am fearfully and wonderfully made. God help me to believe that You have a great and wonderful purpose for my life.

Let us Pray. Journal Below

Journal Entry 17

DATE _____

SCRIPTURES FOR THE DAY

_____

_____

What version of the Bible are you reading?

_____

Does your version of the Bible list out a title for the section you chose to read? Write it out.

_____

_____

FOCUS: Research Question or Topic of Choice

_____

_____

1. Observations → Jeremiah, What Do You See?

Directions: After reading the scriptures for the day, write out 10 or more sentences about what you observed about these scriptures. During this time, <u>try to include two questions to ask God.</u> **Refer back to page 12 to see what you should include in the observations section.

1. What do you notice at first glance about the section you are reading?
2. What names were introduced?
3. What do you notice about the setting?
4. What words are repeated?
5. What words stood out to you?

2. *Interpretation* → Rightly Divide the Word of Truth.

Directions: It is time for you to do research. Dig deep and research the original meaning of the text.

Write at least a 10 sentence interpretation of what you read. Include in your answer what you learned about God, the Holy Spirit, and Jesus! Use your Bible study questions to write out the interpretation. Find articles, online sources, books, and other resources to help you answer questions. **Refer back to page 13 for the full list of information to help you interpret the text.**

While looking for the interpretation, think about the following questions.
History
1. Who wrote the book that you read?
2. What did you learn about the author?
3. Who was the author speaking to in the text?
4. Research some history about the author of the book.
5. What were the **customs and culture** of this time?
6. Which **king was in rule at the time**? What rulings did this king have?
7. Do some research on the **setting**. What did you **learn about the geography of the setting**?
8. **Cross-reference**: What other scriptures relate to the scripture that you read?

Words
1. Look up words that stand out to you, even if it is a simple word.
2. Look up words that you do not know.

Include in your answer:
1. What do you learn about God in this chapter?
2. What do you learn about the Holy Spirit?
3. What do you learn about Jesus?

Write out the interpretation of the section of this text here.

3. General Application → Be a Doer.

General Application: Ask yourself how these scriptures can be applied to the daily life of a Christian.
1. What is the universal lesson that these scriptures teach Christians?
2. What is a Christian principle (truth/idea) that you learned from these scriptures that can be applied to all Christians regardless of their denomination? For example- Jesus is the only way to be in a right relationship with God.
3. What does this scripture or passage help people understand in regards to their purpose, identity, and destiny?

Challenge yourself to write out at least six sentences or more about how this scripture can be applied to the daily life of a Believer in Christ.

4. Personal Application

Take the Plank Out of Your Eye.

Personal Application: Describe what God is trying to teach you through this study.

Ask yourself:
1. How can this scripture be applied to my personal life right now?
2. How do these scriptures personally affect me right now?
3. What is God trying to show me about myself, family, career, destiny, identity, ministry, current issues, etc?

Challenge yourself **to write out six sentences or more.**

5. Action Steps → Faith Without Works is DEAD.

Directions: Write 2-3 next steps that God wants you to take after completing this study. Be specific.

Example: I need to delete my Instagram page <u>because</u> God revealed it is causing me to grumble and complain about my own life. Philippians 2:14 states, "Do everything without grumbling or arguing."

	Action Steps	Why?
1		
2		
3		

6. Prayer → Confess With Your Mouth.

Directions: In this section, you will write out a prayer concerning what God has shown you through the scriptures. Pray about what God is revealing to you about God, Jesus, and the Holy Spirit. Write out a prayer on how He is going to shape your view of Him and how you see yourself.

Write out new biblical declarations or life affirmations that you need to make so that God can help transform you.

Examples: (Based on Psalm 139:14) I declare that I am fearfully and wonderfully made. God help me to believe that You have a great and wonderful purpose for my life.

Let us Pray. Journal Below

Journal Entry 18

DATE _____

SCRIPTURES FOR THE DAY

_____

_____

What version of the Bible are you reading?

_____

Does your version of the Bible list out a title for the section you chose to read? Write it out.

_____

_____

FOCUS: Research Question or Topic of Choice

_____

_____

1. Observations → Jeremiah, What Do You See?

Directions: After reading the scriptures for the day, write out 10 or more sentences about what you observed about these scriptures. During this time, <u>try to include two questions to ask God.</u> **Refer back to page 12 to see what you should include in the observations section.

1. What do you notice at first glance about the section you are reading?
2. What names were introduced?
3. What do you notice about the setting?
4. What words are repeated?
5. What words stood out to you?

2. Interpretation → Rightly Divide the Word of Truth.

Directions: It is time for you to do research. Dig deep and research the original meaning of the text.

Write at least a 10 sentence interpretation of what you read. Include in your answer what you learned about God, the Holy Spirit, and Jesus! Use your Bible study questions to write out the interpretation. Find articles, online sources, books, and other resources to help you answer questions. **Refer back to page 13 for the full list of information to help you interpret the text.**

While looking for the interpretation, think about the following questions.
History
1. Who wrote the book that you read?
2. What did you learn about the author?
3. Who was the author speaking to in the text?
4. Research some history about the author of the book.
5. What were the **customs and culture** of this time?
6. Which **king was in rule at the time**? What rulings did this king have?
7. Do some research on the **setting**. What did you **learn about the geography of the setting**?
8. **Cross-reference**: What other scriptures relate to the scripture that you read?

Words
1. Look up words that stand out to you, even if it is a simple word.
2. Look up words that you do not know.

Include in your answer:
1. What do you learn about God in this chapter?
2. What do you learn about the Holy Spirit?
3. What do you learn about Jesus?

Write out **the interpretation of the section of this text here.**

3. General Application → Be a Doer.

General Application: Ask yourself how these scriptures can be applied to the daily life of a Christian.

1. What is the universal lesson that these scriptures teach Christians?
2. What is a Christian principle (truth/idea) that you learned from these scriptures that can be applied to all Christians regardless of their denomination? For example- Jesus is the only way to be in a right relationship with God.
3. What does this scripture or passage help people understand in regards to their purpose, identity, and destiny?

Challenge yourself **to write out at least six sentences or more about how this scripture can be applied to the daily life of a Believer in Christ.**

4. Personal Application

Take the Plank Out of Your Eye.

Personal Application: Describe what God is trying to teach you through this study.

Ask yourself:
1. How can this scripture be applied to my personal life right now?
2. How do these scriptures personally affect me right now?
3. What is God trying to show me about myself, family, career, destiny, identity, ministry, current issues, etc?

Challenge yourself **to write out six sentences or more.**

5. Action Steps → Faith Without Works is DEAD.

Directions: Write 2-3 next steps that God wants you to take after completing this study. Be specific.

Example: I need to delete my Instagram page <u>because</u> God revealed it is causing me to grumble and complain about my own life. Philippians 2:14 states, "Do everything without grumbling or arguing."

	Action Steps	Why?
1		
2		
3		

6. Prayer → Confess With Your Mouth.

Directions: In this section, you will write out a prayer concerning what God has shown you through the scriptures. Pray about what God is revealing to you about God, Jesus, and the Holy Spirit. Write out a prayer on how He is going to shape your view of Him and how you see yourself.

Write out new biblical declarations or life affirmations that you need to make so that God can help transform you.

Examples: (Based on Psalm 139:14) I declare that I am fearfully and wonderfully made. God help me to believe that You have a great and wonderful purpose for my life.

Let us Pray. Journal Below

Journal Entry 19

DATE _____

SCRIPTURES FOR THE DAY

_____

_____

What version of the Bible are you reading?

_____

Does your version of the Bible list out a title for the section you chose to read? Write it out.

_____

_____

FOCUS: Research Question or Topic of Choice

_____

_____

1. Observations → Jeremiah, What Do You See?

Directions: After reading the scriptures for the day, write out 10 or more sentences about what you observed about these scriptures. During this time, <u>try to include two questions to ask God.</u> **Refer back to page 12 to see what you should include in the observations section.
1. What do you notice at first glance about the section you are reading?
2. What names were introduced?
3. What do you notice about the setting?
4. What words are repeated?
5. What words stood out to you?

2. Interpretation → Rightly Divide the Word of Truth.

Directions: It is time for you to do research. Dig deep and research the original meaning of the text.

Write at least a 10 sentence interpretation of what you read. Include in your answer what you learned about God, the Holy Spirit, and Jesus! Use your Bible study questions to write out the interpretation. Find articles, online sources, books, and other resources to help you answer questions. **Refer back to page 13 for the full list of information to help you interpret the text.**

While looking for the interpretation, think about the following questions.
History
1. Who wrote the book that you read?
2. What did you learn about the author?
3. Who was the author speaking to in the text?
4. Research some history about the author of the book.
5. What were the **customs and culture** of this time?
6. Which **king was in rule at the time**? What rulings did this king have?
7. Do some research on the **setting**. What did you **learn about the geography of the setting**?
8. **Cross-reference**: What other scriptures relate to the scripture that you read?

Words
1. Look up words that stand out to you, even if it is a simple word.
2. Look up words that you do not know.

Include in your answer:
1. What do you learn about God in this chapter?
2. What do you learn about the Holy Spirit?
3. What do you learn about Jesus?

Write out the interpretation of the section of this text here.

3. General Application → Be a Doer.

General Application: Ask yourself how these scriptures can be applied to the daily life of a Christian.

1. What is the universal lesson that these scriptures teach Christians?
2. What is a Christian principle (truth/idea) that you learned from these scriptures that can be applied to all Christians regardless of their denomination? For example- Jesus is the only way to be in a right relationship with God.
3. What does this scripture or passage help people understand in regards to their purpose, identity, and destiny?

Challenge yourself **to write out at least six sentences or more about how this scripture can be applied to the daily life of a Believer in Christ.**

4. Personal Application
Take the Plank Out of Your Eye.

Personal Application: Describe what God is trying to teach you through this study.

Ask yourself:
1. How can this scripture be applied to my personal life right now?
2. How do these scriptures personally affect me right now?
3. What is God trying to show me about myself, family, career, destiny, identity, ministry, current issues, etc?

Challenge yourself **to write out six sentences or more.**

5. Action Steps → Faith Without Works is DEAD.

Directions: Write 2-3 next steps that God wants you to take after completing this study. Be specific.

Example: I need to delete my Instagram page <u>because</u> God revealed it is causing me to grumble and complain about my own life. Philippians 2:14 states, "Do everything without grumbling or arguing."

	Action Steps	Why?
1		
2		
3		

6. Prayer → Confess With Your Mouth.

Directions: In this section, you will write out a prayer concerning what God has shown you through the scriptures. Pray about what God is revealing to you about God, Jesus, and the Holy Spirit. Write out a prayer on how He is going to shape your view of Him and how you see yourself.

Write out new biblical declarations or life affirmations that you need to make so that God can help transform you.

Examples: (Based on Psalm 139:14) I declare that I am fearfully and wonderfully made. God help me to believe that You have a great and wonderful purpose for my life.

Let us Pray. Journal Below

Journal Entry 20   DATE _____

SCRIPTURES FOR THE DAY

_____

_____

What version of the Bible are you reading?

_____

Does your version of the Bible list out a title for the section you chose to read? Write it out.

_____

_____

FOCUS: Research Question or Topic of Choice

_____

_____

1. Observations → Jeremiah, What Do You See?

Directions: After reading the scriptures for the day, write out 10 or more sentences about what you observed about these scriptures. During this time, try to include two questions to ask God. **Refer back to page 12 to see what you should include in the observations section.

1. What do you notice at first glance about the section you are reading?
2. What names were introduced?
3. What do you notice about the setting?
4. What words are repeated?
5. What words stood out to you?

2. Interpretation → Rightly Divide the Word of Truth.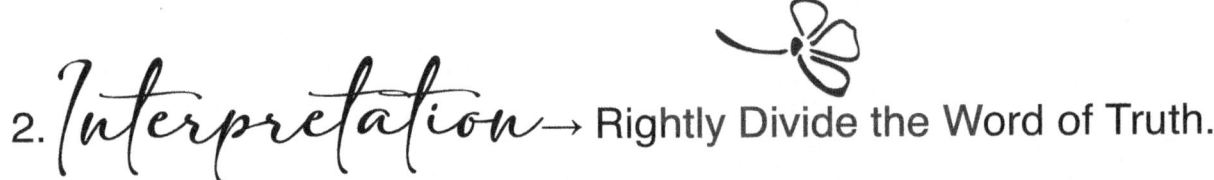

Directions: It is time for you to do research. Dig deep and research the original meaning of the text.

Write at least a 10 sentence interpretation of what you read. Include in your answer what you learned about God, the Holy Spirit, and Jesus! Use your Bible study questions to write out the interpretation. Find articles, online sources, books, and other resources to help you answer questions. **Refer back to page 13 for the full list of information to help you interpret the text.**

While looking for the interpretation, think about the following questions.
History
1. Who wrote the book that you read?
2. What did you learn about the author?
3. Who was the author speaking to in the text?
4. Research some history about the author of the book.
5. What were the **customs and culture** of this time?
6. Which **king was in rule at the time**? What rulings did this king have?
7. Do some research on the **setting**. What did you **learn about the geography of the setting**?
8. **Cross-reference**: What other scriptures relate to the scripture that you read?

Words
1. Look up words that stand out to you, even if it is a simple word.
2. Look up words that you do not know.

Include in your answer:
1. What do you learn about God in this chapter?
2. What do you learn about the Holy Spirit?
3. What do you learn about Jesus?

Write out the interpretation of the section of this text here.

3. *General Application* → Be a Doer.

General Application: Ask yourself how these scriptures can be applied to the daily life of a Christian.
1. What is the universal lesson that these scriptures teach Christians?
2. What is a Christian principle (truth/idea) that you learned from these scriptures that can be applied to all Christians regardless of their denomination? For example- Jesus is the only way to be in a right relationship with God.
3. What does this scripture or passage help people understand in regards to their purpose, identity, and destiny?

Challenge yourself **to write out at least six sentences or more about how this scripture can be applied to the daily life of a Believer in Christ.**

4. Personal Application
Take the Plank Out of Your Eye.

Personal Application: Describe what God is trying to teach you through this study.

Ask yourself:
1. How can this scripture be applied to my personal life right now?
2. How do these scriptures personally affect me right now?
3. What is God trying to show me about myself, family, career, destiny, identity, ministry, current issues, etc?

Challenge yourself **to write out six sentences or more.**

5. Action Steps → Faith Without Works is DEAD.

Directions: Write 2-3 next steps that God wants you to take after completing this study. Be specific.

Example: I need to delete my Instagram page <u>because</u> God revealed it is causing me to grumble and complain about my own life. Philippians 2:14 states, "Do everything without grumbling or arguing."

	Action Steps	**Why?**
1		
2		
3		

6. Prayer → Confess With Your Mouth.

Directions: In this section, you will write out a prayer concerning what God has shown you through the scriptures. Pray about what God is revealing to you about God, Jesus, and the Holy Spirit. Write out a prayer on how He is going to shape your view of Him and how you see yourself.

Write out new biblical declarations or life affirmations that you need to make so that God can help transform you.

Examples: (Based on Psalm 139:14) I declare that I am fearfully and wonderfully made. God help me to believe that You have a great and wonderful purpose for my life.

Let us Pray. Journal Below

Journal Entry 21   DATE _____

SCRIPTURES FOR THE DAY

_____

_____

What version of the Bible are you reading?

_____

Does your version of the Bible list out a title for the section you chose to read? Write it out.

_____

_____

FOCUS: Research Question or Topic of Choice

_____

_____

1. Observations → Jeremiah, What Do You See?

Directions: After reading the scriptures for the day, write out 10 or more sentences about what you observed about these scriptures. During this time, <u>try to include two questions to ask God.</u> **Refer back to page 12 to see what you should include in the observations section.

1. What do you notice at first glance about the section you are reading?
2. What names were introduced?
3. What do you notice about the setting?
4. What words are repeated?
5. What words stood out to you?

2. Interpretation → Rightly Divide the Word of Truth.

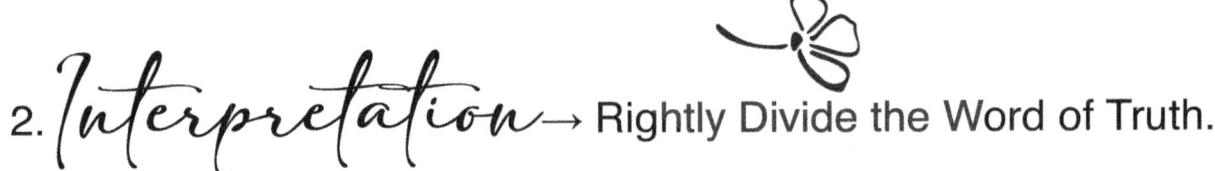

Directions: It is time for you to do research. Dig deep and research the original meaning of the text.

Write at least a 10 sentence interpretation of what you read. Include in your answer what you learned about God, the Holy Spirit, and Jesus! Use your Bible study questions to write out the interpretation. Find articles, online sources, books, and other resources to help you answer questions. **Refer back to page 13 for the full list of information to help you interpret the text.**

While looking for the interpretation, think about the following questions.
History
1. Who wrote the book that you read?
2. What did you learn about the author?
3. Who was the author speaking to in the text?
4. Research some history about the author of the book.
5. What were the **customs and culture** of this time?
6. Which **king was in rule at the time**? What rulings did this king have?
7. Do some research on the **setting**. What did you **learn about the geography of the setting**?
8. **Cross-reference**: What other scriptures relate to the scripture that you read?

Words
1. Look up words that stand out to you, even if it is a simple word.
2. Look up words that you do not know.

Include in your answer:
1. What do you learn about God in this chapter?
2. What do you learn about the Holy Spirit?
3. What do you learn about Jesus?

Write out the interpretation of the section of this text here.

3. General Application → Be a Doer.

General Application: Ask yourself how these scriptures can be applied to the daily life of a Christian.

1. What is the universal lesson that these scriptures teach Christians?
2. What is a Christian principle (truth/idea) that you learned from these scriptures that can be applied to all Christians regardless of their denomination? For example- Jesus is the only way to be in a right relationship with God.
3. What does this scripture or passage help people understand in regards to their purpose, identity, and destiny?

Challenge yourself **to write out at least six sentences or more about how this scripture can be applied to the daily life of a Believer in Christ.**

4. Personal Application
Take the Plank Out of Your Eye.

Personal Application: Describe what God is trying to teach you through this study.

Ask yourself:
1. How can this scripture be applied to my personal life right now?
2. How do these scriptures personally affect me right now?
3. What is God trying to show me about myself, family, career, destiny, identity, ministry, current issues, etc?

Challenge yourself **to write out six sentences or more.**

5. Action Steps → Faith Without Works is DEAD.

Directions: Write 2-3 next steps that God wants you to take after completing this study. Be specific.

Example: I need to delete my Instagram page <u>because</u> God revealed it is causing me to grumble and complain about my own life. Philippians 2:14 states, "Do everything without grumbling or arguing."

	Action Steps	Why?
1		
2		
3		

6. Prayer → Confess With Your Mouth.

Directions: In this section, you will write out a prayer concerning what God has shown you through the scriptures. Pray about what God is revealing to you about God, Jesus, and the Holy Spirit. Write out a prayer on how He is going to shape your view of Him and how you see yourself.

Write out new biblical declarations or life affirmations that you need to make so that God can help transform you.

Examples: (Based on Psalm 139:14) I declare that I am fearfully and wonderfully made. God help me to believe that You have a great and wonderful purpose for my life.

Let us Pray. Journal Below

About the Author

Tokunbo Okulaja is a first-generation American born to Nigerian parents. She grew up both in Prince George's County Maryland and Fairfax, Virginia. She graduated with a Bachelor of Arts degree in Government and Politics with a minor in Rhetoric from the University of Maryland, College Park. Tokunbo Okulaja also completed her Master of Arts degree in Public School Building Leadership from Teachers College, Columbia University in New York.

In 2013, Tokunbo joined Teach For America. This began her ongoing career in teaching middle school English, language arts, reading, social studies, and leadership in both public and charter school settings. Tokunbo served as a lead teacher in underserved communities in Mississippi, Louisiana, Illinois, and North Carolina for seven years. Because of her dedication to developing young leaders, she became the founder of Redeem the Teens Global Ministries. Their first initiative is the When Gentlemen Speak program, where they focus on equipping young, Black males to excel in academics, character, and entrepreneurship.

In 2019, Tokunbo became the CEO and founder of Tokunbo The Leader LLC. Tokunbo The Leader LLC is designed to help leaders discover VIP (Voice, Identity, and Purpose) so that they can dominate in their destiny! She currently resides in North Carolina where she continues blazing trails in the area of education.

Learn More at
tokunbotheleader.com!

Stay connected with Tokunbo and learn how to use your writing and leadership gift by reading blogs, receiving updates on courses, and so much *more!*

Keep in touch. Let us know how this journal has helped you on *your* journey of studying the *Bible*.

Email info@tokunbotheleader.com

f Tokunbo The Leader

◙ tokunbotheleader

▶ Tokunbo The Leader

Made in the USA
Monee, IL
28 April 2026